LASTINGHAM

text © ELIZABETH LESTER

drawings © ROSEMARY ROBERTS

ISBN   0 9535072 4 6

AD2000

Published by The Blackthorn Press
Blackthorn House
Middleton Road
Pickering YO18 8AL

CONTENTS

ACKNOWLEDGEMENTS

This book is derived from notes and records collected by Elizabeth Lester over many years, and from contributions made, among others, by Mabs Biggins, John Bulmer, Lily Campion, Andie Cattle, Harold Dobson, Barbara Doughty, Bertram Frank, Douglas Gohl, Raymond Hayes, Ralph Lester, John Makepeace, Florrie Pape, Martha Rex, Richard Leigh Perkins, Nigel Roberts, Rosemary Roberts, Gillian Smith, Tom Strickland, Dulcie Swales, Ray Taylor and Pat Wood. The drawings are by Rosemary Roberts. Thanks are due to all who contributed, and to Nigel and Rosemary Roberts who got the material ready for printing.

No history of Lastingham could be written without extensive reference to:
   Historia Rievallensis by Rev W Eastmead   (1824)
   History of the Ancient Parish of Lastingham
                   by Rev F H Weston (1914)

Both are books of lasting value, and they are recommended to the interested reader for further study.

In Lestingeham. hb̄ Gamel .i. man̄ cu .i. car̄
ruca... ad gt̄d. N̄c de Bertn̄ h̄t abb̄ ibi .i. uillm̄
cu .i. car̄.
In Spauntun. hb̄ Gamel .i. manq̄ cu .vi. caruca
ras̄... 7 dimid ad gt̄d. N̄c h̄t abb̄ de Bertn̄. In dn̄io
.ii. car̄ 7 xc. uill cu .ii. car̄. Silua past̄ dimid lev l̄g
7 iii. q̄rent̄ lat. T.R.E. ualb x. sot̄. m̄ similit̄.

Lastingham and Spaunton

in Domesday Book

CHAPTER ONE

Origins

The underlying Jurassic rocks of the Lastingham area, on the southern edge of the North York Moors, were formed about 150 million years ago. There is evidènce that the area may have escaped glaciation during the last Ice Age, remaining as an isolated peak of snow-covered rock above the surrounding ice.

Around ten thousand years ago, as the ice melted, the emerging vegetation was probably a rich oak-birch forest, with alders beside the becks. On the high windswept moors the tree cover would have been scrubby, with hardy birches and pines, rowan, low under-shrubs and ling.

Britain was severed from the Continent at the end of the Ice Age. The Vale of Pickering, scoured and filled by melting ice, became swampy and traces of lakeland dwellings have been discovered in the Vale dating from about 8000BC, while prehistoric animal bones have been found at nearby Kirkdale.

Flint Age and Stone Age Man were succeeded by Bronze Age Man and moorland burial sites have been found at Loose Howe and Obtrusen Rigg. The forest was cleared from the Bronze Age onwards, and by mediaeval times the vegetation was much as it is at present. Since the Middle Ages the moors have been used for sheep grazing and the dale as pasture land.

When man had learnt how to smelt iron, possibly around the middle of the sixth century BC, currency was introduced in place of barter. The production of cloth, farming, a strong artistic tradition and a social hierarchy, together with various religious practices, all developed in England. There was also a writing system called Ogham, coming from Ireland and Wales, which survived to co-exist with Latin in Roman times.

Two of the principal tribes in Yorkshire in the ensuing Iron Age were the peaceable Parisii (east Yorkshire, Holderness and Humberside), and the more warlike Brigantes, who claimed the Pennine areas to the west and north. Smaller tribes were driven into the hilly areas of the moors between the two, and Lastingham seems to have been more or less on the border.

The Celtic Inheritance

It is now well accepted that the Celtic people came to this country as traders and settlers over a long period of time from about 700BC, and gradually absorbed the indigenous population into the Celtic culture. Our knowledge of that culture comes from burial sites, hill forts and other enclosures. As might be expected, we find the hilly areas of the moors, including Lastingham, more thinly populated than the lowland areas.

There are no hill forts documented for the immediate area round Lastingham, though the frequent discovery of arrowheads suggests that it may have been a good hunting area. Stone circles have been documented at Cawthorne, Levisham and Blakey Ridge. Iron ore was mined at Rosedale; no smelting seems to have been done there, though there is evidence of iron being worked in a bloomery on Levisham Moor dating from some thousand years earlier than any other in the area. Carts and chariots have been found at Cawthorne, suggesting that there must have been considerable activity, even though the area was apparently not thickly populated.

It is interesting to note that when the Romans left, and Britain became prey to invaders, many Celtic people left for Europe (giving their name to Brittany in northern France) to return in 1066 with the Norman Conquest - an example of the cross-migration that had been going on for centuries.

Romans

By AD74 the Romans had conquered most of the country. Catterick (Cateractonium) became a local capital, and Malton (Derventio) was founded. During the second century the town of Malton (protecting York from the east) was rebuilt entirely in stone, but later its importance was reduced. By contrast, York gained in importance, developing an agrarian economy during the third century, with a prosperous civilian population.

However, remains of Roman villas have been found at Rudstone and Beadlam, and substantial grain stores at Malton. A stone cist (chest) was discovered at Spaunton early in the

twentieth century, containing a skeleton and small urn with food remains. It seems possible that the cist may be linked to the Romano-British farmstead near Ings Balk. Soon after 280 the first Saxon invasions caused the Romans to evacuate the area, and the grain stores were burned.

The early part of the fourth century appears to have been relatively peaceful. There were Roman signal stations on the York/Scarborough road, and a military camp at Cawthorne near Pickering. A small encampment 1.5 miles north east of Lastingham (near the forester's cottage on the Rosedale road) of about 1 acre, was possibly used for tending cattle.

The Romans allowed Angles and Saxons to migrate from the Continent because they were useful, and by the middle of the fifth century Deira (most of present day Yorkshire) was partly inhabited by Saxon mercenaries in Roman employment. Following further less welcome invasion by Angles and Saxons, and incursions by Picts from the north, there was a gradual withdrawal by the Romans into southern Britain, and the north was left to fend for itself. The Anglo-Saxons were of course pagan, with a pagan priesthood, and ruled by noblemen who maintained their authority with large displays of wealth.

The Dark Ages

By the sixth century, the whole area seems to have become a permanent battle-ground, as king fought king for possession of the territory. Some were pagan and some Christian. The first king on record was Aelle, king of Deira, in 558. He killed one Ragner Lothbrok, whose sons later avenged their father's death by murdering Aelle in York.

Violence continued into the seventh century. King Penda of Mercia killed Oswald, king of Deira. Oswald's brother Oswy subsequently killed Penda. Oswald's son was Athelwald, and it was he who granted land at Lastingham to Cedd, a monk from Lindisfarne.

Oswald's daughter, Hilda, was the first abbess of Whitby, having been given to the church by her father in gratitude for victory over Penda. Cedd, Chad, Celin and Cynebil were four brothers educated by St Aidan at Lindisfarne. Until 652, Cedd was in Mercia at the court of King Penda. He was then sent to Essex where the king of the East Saxons, Sigbert the Good, had been converted to Christianity, and he was joined by Cynebil. Cedd was then created Bishop of the East Saxons in 654. On one of his frequent visits to Lindisfarne Cedd became known to Athelwald, king of Deira, at whose court Celin was a priest.

Athelwald asked Cedd to accept a grant of land on which to build a monastery to which Athelwald could come to pray, and where he could be buried when he died. Cedd's original church and monastery buildings were made of wood, and must have been on or near to the site of the present church. But not long after the foundation of his monastery at Lastingham, Cedd contracted the plague (then rife in the country) and died, together with the twelve brothers at the monastery.

Cedd was succeeded by his brother Chad, who assumed full charge of the monastery (presumably re-populated), and having been consecrated Bishop of York, retired to Lastingham in 669, the victim of church politics. Soon afterwards he became Bishop of Lichfield where he lived with seven or eight brothers from Lastingham until his death in 672.

There is a well in Front Street, Lastingham, which is dedicated to St Cedd and one in High Street dedicated to St Chad. There is a third well in Low Street, which is named after St Ovin (Owine), who gave up a powerful position at the royal court to join the monastery as a manual worker when Chad was abbot.

The three wells

The original wooden monastery church was eventually replaced by one of stone. Fragments can still be seen in the crypt of the present church. Originally lay people were not allowed into the church, but gathered round the preaching cross outside to hear the priest. The proportions of these great Saxon crosses were about 1 across to 6 down, and Lastingham's great cross would have been about 27 feet high - the largest pre-Norman monument in the country. There was also a smaller cross which would have been about 12 feet high.

In the new building St Cedd's body was removed from its burial place outside, and placed on the right, or Gospel, side of the altar.

There is no record of other dwellings in Lastingham, though the monastery must have attracted lay people into the vicinity. It was in such monasteries, on the fringes of Europe, that the spark of civilisation was kept alive in the West during the Dark Ages, until the rebirth of learning in mediaeval times.

Early References and the Danish Invasions

The earliest written reference to Lastingham is in Bede's *Ecclesiastical History*, written in 731, which refers to the foundation of a monastery by Cedd. Alcuin of York, who was born in 735, wrote of Lastingham:

'In this desolate spot where there had been none but beasts, and men living in the fashion of beasts, the fruit of good works should be brought forth'.[1]

The 8th century *Anglo-Saxon Chronicle* records the first of the Danish invasions:

'The ravaging of heathen men lamentably destroyed God's church at Lindisfarne through rapine and slaughter'.

---

(1) from 'Versus de paribus, regibus et sanctis Eboracensis Ecclesiae'.
The passage is quoted from Ecclesiastes.

Alcuin wrote at the same time:

> 'Never before has such terror appeared in Britain as we have now suffered from a pagan race'.

The invasions continued well into the next century, and in 867 the brothers Ingua and Hubba sailed from Denmark to destroy Whitby and penetrate further inland to pillage the villages of Hackness and Lastingham.

All such early records of the Viking invasions were of course the work of the clergy - there were no other scholars. They were rightly afraid of and scandalised by the destruction of the accessible and undefended religious houses.

Modern research suggests that the Vikings were no better and no worse than any other invaders of those times. Christian missionaries had already penetrated Scandinavia, and there is evidence that Viking settlers in Britain showed some respect for the sacred places, and within a generation were erecting Christian funerary monuments over their dead in Yorkshire. In 867 Halfden the Dane decreed a peaceful division of the land, and by 886 the land between the Tees and the Humber was divided into Thryddings (i.e. thirds or ridings).

The presence of a hogback coffin and a cross shaft found near the church at Lastingham suggests that there was some co-existence of pagan with Christian beliefs, and possibly conversion, allowing the monastery to remain a place of worship and sanctity.

The hill descending to Lastingham from the

named from the Viking words for 'steep steps', but we have no record of events at Lastingham during this period. There was no shortage of activity in the surrounding area as Anglo-Saxons and Vikings fought for control. Ripon Minster was burned down in 947. During the 36 years between 919 and 955, York was captured by Ragnald, a Viking from Norway, re-captured by Edward the Elder (King of Wessex and Alfred the Great's son), lost again to the Vikings, re-captured by Athelstan (Edward's son), lost again to Olaf, a Viking from Dublin, re-captured by Edmund (Athelstan's brother), and threatened by Eric Bloodaxe who was expelled twice by Eadred (also Athelstan's brother).

By the end of the century the Vikings were wearing down resistance to their presence. When we next hear of Lastingham, the church is in ruins.

The Crypt Stones and the Vikings

The earliest of the crypt stones in the church of St Mary (once called St Peter's) in Lastingham is the late 7th century gable filial. A finely carved door jamb, a smaller cross head, and an abbot's chair (which at the time of writing is on loan to the Yorkshire Museum in York) all date from the 8th century. From later in the same century there is a large cross head, a cross arm and another fragment together with a second door jamb from the 9th century.

The sculpting of stone continued throughout the period of both Anglo-Saxon and Viking prominence. From the Viking period the cross shafts, the cross head and the hogback all date from the 10th century.

The Lastingham carvings appear to be of stone from the Aislaby quarries near Whitby. The stone would have been transported across the moors along Wade's Causeway (the Roman road running south from the quarries to the camp at Cawthorne, then on to the other Aislaby in the Vale of Pickering and to Amotherby, west of Malton). Sandstone carvings similar to the Lastingham ones can be found in the churches at Kirkdale, Sinnington and Middleton.

Viking workmanship is somewhat cruder than that of the Saxons, and some of the symbols are different, such as those on the hogback, but the Christian cross shafts and head do suggest some continuity. There is no evidence of any deliberate destruction of the monastery, and although it was abandoned we should not assume that this must have been due to the Viking invasion. The continuity of the carved stones suggests that the church itself may have been in use throughout the Saxon and Viking periods. We cannot know how dilapidated local churches had become by the 11th century, but it is interesting that both Saxon and Viking carved stones were included in the finished Norman churches.

St Mary Church Lastingham has a Saxon mass dial in the first buttress to the east of the porch on the south wall, and a fragment of another dial forms part of the exterior of the south west tower buttress.

Domesday

There is no further record of Lastingham until the Norman Conquest. By mid-October of 1066, William the Conqueror had brought Norman rule to Britain, and the best remembered achievement of his twenty-one years is the Domesday Book, in which both *Spanton* and *Lestingham* are mentioned.

Tradition says that William himself came to the area during the harrying of the North, when he succeeded in subduing the warring factions of outlying areas. Lost in the snow on the moors between Bransdale and Westerdale he is said to have sworn and shouted 'like Billyo' while looking for the rest of his troops! But after the harrying of the North, not a man is said to have been left alive between the Humber and the Tees.

Land values were low in these hilly areas of mostly moor and forest. In 1078, Stephen, Abbot of Whitby, sought leave of William to move to the vacant monastery at Lastingham, as he had lost the protection of Lord William Percy, and was thus prey to the Norse pirates and the inland outlaws. Afterwards Stephen wrote:

'In the King's Demesne not far from Whitteby, there was a place called Lastingham, then indeed vacant, but formerly noted for the number and piety of the monks there. This place was given us by the King, and we began to restore it by degrees, and to erect such buildings as were necessary for a habitation of monks'.

In fact they rebuilt the crypt, and above it erected an eastern apse, a choir, a transept, the base for a tower and the foundation for a nave to the west, before deciding that the neighbourhood was no safer than Whitby. They moved on to York to found what became St Mary's Abbey. But it seems likely that Lastingham church continued to be used from time to time, served from St Mary's. Certainly the work done by Stephen is incorporated in the present building.

the crypt

William had in the meantime given Stephen the lordship of the manor of Spaunton with the same amount of land as Gamel, lord of Kirkdale, owned; and Stephen also acquired from Berenger de Todeni 'one villein with one plough'.

Spaunton Forest

By the 14th century, the manor included the forest of Spaunton, described in 1328 as 'between the rivers Dove and Seven' and between 'the boundary of Cleveland to the road leading through Catthwait from Pickering to Helmsley'. The game in the forest belonged to the Crown until 1335 when the king agreed to transfer the gaming rights to the Abbot of St Mary's in exchange for other interests, but only after ascertaining that the game was not very plentiful!

Earlier in the century the area had been visited on a hunting expedition by Edward II - the only royal visit recorded until modern times.

The lordship of the manor remained with the successive abbots of St Mary's until Henry VIII's suppression of the monasteries in the 1530s.

CHAPTER TWO

12th century

The Battle of the Standard at Thirsk between King Stephen and King David of Scotland in 1138 marks a local involvement in the Scottish incursions which occurred from time to time during the 12th and 13th centuries.

The accession of Henry II (1154) affected the village of Lastingham, when additions were made to the land of the manor. The common people's rights of grazing, and taking turf and wood still remained, to provide some sustenance for those too poor to survive without them.

When Richard I came to the throne in 1189, taxes were levied to pay for the crusades, and many people joined his forces in the hope of reaping rich rewards.

Although there is a lack of local information relating to this period, one legend runs as follows:

'A vile baron named Eustace destroyed Spaunton Castle and despoiled its noble possessions while the Lady Elfleda's betrothed lord was absent on a crusade. Being forewarned, the Lady Elfleda got Baron Spanton to assign all his property to the absent Gamel; and after her death her spirit was permitted to watch over the ruined castle, below which the title deeds were deposited until Gamel's return'.

There is in fact no record of Gamel at this time, and Spaunton was not a real castle - merely a small manor house surrounded by a crenellated wall of stone and lime with a moat - though castle was a term which was used for any such fortified house.

13th Century

Between 1208 and 1212 Pope Innocent III imposed an Interdict on all England, due to a dispute between the Pope and King John. This was to affect everyone in the land - there would be no celebration of mass, confessions would be held at the church door, and the dead would be buried in ditches instead of in consecrated ground.

In 1215 the priest Cozoni was appointed specifically to serve Lastingham. His official description as Scriptor to the Pope suggests that some importance must have been attached to the parish. At this time the population of Yorkshire was about 11,000 and there were 12 nunneries and 8 monasteries already in existence.

Grants of land in other parts of the parish were acquired by St Mary's Abbey, and it continued to control the manor under the system of socage (letting off tracts of land to various people). By 1230 we find the Abbey appointing the first endowed vicar, de Sefton, to Lastingham. There are records of there being a tannery in the village at this time.

14th Century

This was the century of the Hundred Years War, paid for out of new taxes and straining the economy, of the Peasants Revolt, and of the Black Death, which reached a peak between 1348-9 when 17-25% of the population died. As a result of the plague, work was plentiful and wages rose by 50%.

Lastingham appears to have remained quiet. The church was improved by the addition of windows and new aisles, the south aisle being demolished and rebuilt in the Decorated style. We have records of the vicars appointed, and some testamentary evidence of local people. In 1393 John of Croxton's will showed that he bequeathed:

'to Sir Symond of Lastingham[1] *3s.4d. and 3 ells*[2] *of cloth for a gown; also I will to Elyn that dwells in Lastingham 3s.4d. and 3 ells of blanket; also I will to Alice of Lastingham 2s. and russet cloth to make her a cloke. Also 6s.8d. to the Nunnery of Keldhome, and two torches 9 feet long to Lastingham Church and two torches 9 feet long to Rosedale Abbey.*[3]

16th Century

This was the great Tudor century, and a time when the spirit of progress and adventure was high. By then the Renaissance had brought about cultural changes, two of which were of great importance to the common people.

These were William Tyndale's translation of the bible into the vernacular, and the under-rated achievement of Roger Ascham's standardisation of spelling, giving everyone the opportunity to read and write instead of this being the prerogative of the few. New lands were discovered, and new knowledge and wealth was brought to many with the expansion of trade. Prices rose and extra bullion was produced. In England the population doubled by the end of the century. The effects of these changes were not felt immediately but continual conflict

---

(1) 'Sir' denotes that Symond was in holy orders.
(2) An ell is a little more than a metre.
(3) The extract is taken from Testamenta Eboracensia,
Surtees Society, No. 148.

with the French, the Spanish, the Scots, the Irish and, of course, the Church of Rome, eventually affected everyone in one way or another.

With the change in tenancy terms and in sheep farming together with the disappearance of the manorial open field system, it is not known if anyone in Lastingham lost a livelihood, but people may well have suffered.

By the middle of the century, however, we can be more certain about what happened. In 1544 Henry VIII married Catherine Parr, whose family lived nearby at Sinnington. He reinstated Mary and Elizabeth as his rightful heirs.

In 1550 the Manor at Spaunton was either bought by or given to Lord Grey de Wilton. (At about the same time, the Darley family bought Aldby Park at Buttercrambe). Happily the rights of the Spaunton Commoners and the Court Leet were preserved and are still with us today.

In 1536, at the time of the dissolution of the monasteries, the English church became the King's by attainder, i.e. surrender. Lastingham church must have had an annual income of more than £200 per annum, since those with less were automatically dissolved. The tithes remained with the Archbishop of York. The church, too, should have passed to him, but due to a clerical error it was described as being in Spaunton, which actually has no church of its own, so it remained with the Crown.

In 1542 there were about 80 families living in the parish, and the parish registers show that increasing numbers of people arrived to operate local glass furnaces between about 1570 and 1600. But the Elizabethan economy operated on the monopoly system (producing under licence), and when Sir John Bowes was granted the monopoly he speedily closed down those furnaces which were operating illegally. Presumably the glass-workers were forced to seek subsistence elsewhere.

Poor Laws were passed requiring each parish to appoint 'Overseers of the Poor'. The Elizabethan Poor Law legislation was an attempt to deal with the increasing numbers of beggars and vagrants who wandered about the country and, under the provisions of that legislation, Lastingham came under the jurisdiction of Pickering.

St. Mary's church registers date from 1559 and from them we know that Thomas Ferries, who gave the village its first school, was born in Lastingham in 1568 and became Lord Mayor of Hull. The Rev Eastmead writing in 1824 describes a coat-of-arms, badly worn but still discernible hanging in the church, which he thinks belonged to the Ferries family.

17th Century

This period is remembered by everyone for the Civil War leading to the Commonwealth of 1649-1660, the Great Plague of 1665 and the Great Fire of London in 1666, but Lastingham seems to have been spared the fate which had struck St. Cedd and his followers so many years before. Other small villages, such as the plague struck Eyam in Derbyshire, were not so fortunate.

The Civil War and the Commonwealth were, however, another matter - everyone in England was affected. Apart from the enforced alterations in religious observance, many people must have been recruited as soldiers, or have seen or heard marching feet, drum-beats or the rumble and creaking of wagons and gun-carriages. Did anyone come to Lastingham village seeking fodder for the horses or meat for the men? Nearby, Scarborough Castle was under siege by Cromwell's men for 17 months in 1644-5.

During those troubled times nothing very constructive was done in Lastingham. In 1617 a chalice was given to the church, and in 1620 Thomas Ferries, now a wealthy and respectable man after his brief flirtation with piracy on the high seas, 'new-builded' the church and set up a free school in the village, (which functioned until 1743). Nothing else was done to the church until 1663, when a second bell was installed in the tower. (In 1735, a tenor bell was hung - bringing the total to three - and in 1813 the smallest bell, the treble, was replaced).

All was not completely peaceful in the village however. The vicar, Leonard Conyers, seems to have kept the Quarter Sessions busy. His stormy ministry lasted from 1637 to 1662 and he somehow survived the Puritan era as 'vicar' until 1649 and 'minister' until 1660, by not allowing Phillip Peckett, the

Puritan appointee of the Commonwealth, into the vicarage!

It must have been a trying time for everyone, for after Archbishop Laud was beheaded in 1645 no burial services were allowed, the Book of Common Prayer was forbidden and there were no holidays except Christmas Day.

William Cheeseman, whose family had lived in Lastingham for many years, rivalled Leonard Conyers in court appearances: At Helmsley Quarter Sessions 10.7.1606:

> *'William Cheeseman and his wife, of Lastingham, to hold no converse with Katherine Wilson, late of Lastingham, Spinster, before the next assizes. The latter to be in the custodie of Thomas Sheppard, of Hutton-le-Hole'.*

At Thirsk Quarter Sessions 11 & 12.7.1609:

> *'William Allan and William Cheeseman, for brewing etc.'*

At Helmsley Quarter Sessions, 1611:

> *'Will. Cheeseman, late of Lastingham, yeoman and Susanna, his wife, for abusing and threatening, at Helmsley'.*

William Allen was summoned again in 1610 not only for brewing, but also for *'suffering play at cards in his house'*, and Christopher Hall was summoned for brewing.

In 1603 certain rules, called canons, had been drawn up by royal authority for the guidance of the Church. Canon 87 provides:

> *'The Archbishops and all Bishops..... shall procure..... a true note and terrier of all the glebes, lands, meadows, gardens, orchards, houses, stocks, implements, tenements, and portions of tithes lying out of their parishes which belong to any parsonage vicarage.....to be taken by the view of honest men in every parish.....and to be laid up in the Bishop's registry; there to be for a perpetual memory thereof'.*

The earliest terrier that has been found for Lastingham is dated 1685, and terriers are still prepared every five years by the Churchwardens for the information of the Diocese.

Meanwhile in 1653, under the Protectorate of Oliver Cromwell, every parish was required to appoint a Registrar to keep proper records, and George Pierson was the first to be appointed for Lastingham.

CHAPTER THREE

Eighteenth Century Village Life

A typical 18th century village would contain not more than about 300 people, and the 19th century census returns for the township of Lastingham (without Spaunton) show an average population of about 175.

There would usually be a squire or lord of the manor, and a parson, each of whom might employ a number of the unmarried villagers as servants. In the manor of Spaunton there would in addition be one or two freehold or copyhold farmers, with cottagers and labourers and specialist workers (blacksmith, thatcher and others), who would have rights of grazing, turbary etc if they had no facilities of their own; also a number of un-attached old and young, widows and orphans, living with re-lations or in cottages or almshouses, and maintained partly or wholly by the Poor Rate levied on the better off.

The occupation and use of the village lands were still controlled by the manorial court or, in the case of Lastingham, by the Court Leet, though most of the Court's other functions had by the 18th century been taken over by the Vestry (i.e.the Constable and Churchwardens and such of the inhabitants as attended meetings). Apart from the control of land use, the four main functions of village government were the responsibility of unpaid officers. These officers were the Constable, responsible for keeping the peace, the Surveyor of Highways who main-tained roads and bridges, the Churchwardens who were respon-sible for keeping in repair the approaches to the church and its fabric and the 'Overseers of the Poor' who made provision for the poor.

Inhabitants tried to have substitutes appointed where possible, especially to the office of Constable, who was appointed by the Justices, or by the Court Leet when operative. The Constable had immense powers of interference over the rest of the villagers, but was answerable to the Justices for the maintenance of order. He was also responsible for looking after any alehouses, and calling parish meetings.

The Overseers of the Poor and the Churchwardens were elected annually from among the local inhabitants. The Overseers of the Poor had the most important duty of seeing that no stranger obtained a settlement (and thus a share in the right to poor relief in the village) - hence their very severe treatment of people accused of vagrancy.

The Churchwardens levied the church rate for defraying their expenses, and were responsible for collecting the moneys authorised by statute and assessed at Quarter Sessions. They would be supported in their duties by the Justices, Squire and Vicar, who would levy distraint on defaulters through the Constable.

The Churchwardens also had to report to the Ordinary (a cleric appointed by the diocese) during his annual visit, on the incumbent, the church and its furniture, the vicarage and churchyard, and on the moral and religious behaviour of the people. (These are still duties of the Churchwardens - apart perhaps from the last item!)

The Surveyor of Highways was selected by the Justices from a list of nominees submitted by the Vestry. The Justices authorised the Highway Rate, and passed the Surveyor's accounts (or not as the case may be).

The Surveyor of Highways directed the maintenance of the highways in which all the people were legally bound to assist, giving 6 days a year to the job. The Surveyor of Highways also collected the default fines, and cash payments in lieu of work. The parish was collectively responsible, and if the work was not done to the satisfaction of Quarter Sessions or the Assizes the parish was liable to a fine which would become a heavy additional rate. Road work was strongly resented and often neglected, so that roads were sometimes barely usable until the Turnpike Acts in the late seventeenth and early eighteenth centuries.

Mutual co-operation between these unpaid officers (who in small villages must have held more than one office at once) made them very powerful, but their jobs were onerous and made the holders even more the servants of the squire and parson (who would usually be the Justices) than were the other villagers.

A number of minor paid officers worked under the unpaid officials - especially the Parish Clerk, who was appointed for life, with the benefit of customary fees and dues. There was also a Dog Whipper, whose business was to quieten the dogs brought into church by worshippers during the service.

The authority of the parson had declined by the eighteenth century, but respect for his cloth and education and his position still gave him wide powers of interference. He had legal authority to examine the 'characters' of servants when they changed jobs (an annual event), and to certify passes for those leaving their place of settlement to work elsewhere.

Beating The Bounds of the Parish

This took place around Whitsuntide and was an annual event until 1764. The purpose of beating the bounds was to establish the exact position of the parish boundary.

The historian S D Kennedy wrote:

'A procession headed by the vicar and the principal men of the parish on horseback, each of whom carried a willow wand and accompanied by boys, set out to visit the parish boundaries. In order to impress them on the minds of the unfortunate urchins, it was customary to bump them against the marking stones or to apply the willow wands to their backs. If a river or stream served as a boundary the boys were thrown into it as well. The bounds and the boys having been duly beaten, the party returned home and all went to a service in church.'

18th Century in Lastingham

Not much is known about Lastingham during the earlier part of this century.

In 1740, Joseph Foord, the Surveyor from Kirkbymoorside, drew up an ambitious scheme for draining a large area of moorland and channeling the water. A survey was carried out and one or two channels dug, but the scheme was never completed.

With the coming of the 1770s however, there was a surge of activity. During the next thirty years the American War of Independence and the French Revolution both impinged upon local life. American ships were sailing off the Yorkshire coast with hostile intent, and the French Revolution gave rise to fears that a similar uprising might start here. With such uncertainty about, young men left the village to walk to Whitby in the hope of going to sea. The navy's press gangs were operating in the town, and privateers were sailing up and down so that protected convoys had to be formed in the North Sea - but it was the whaling fleets which were the young men's objective.

The whaling captain Crispin Bean retired to Lastingham in 1790, having made his fortune as master of the *Henrietta*, and later Captain Jackson arrived having been master of the *John*. A young lad from Cropton became the famous Captain Scoresby, who is credited with inventing the crow's nest. Whaling was important to the economies of many families - the men going off for the summer season and returning to farming for the rest of the year.

Between 1771 and 1789 the foundations to those parts of the original monastery next to the church, which were begun but never finished, were demolished (this implies that they were of some height) by the local people in order to repair and build their own properties. The following extract is from Eastmead's book:

'About 50 years since the foundations of the monastery were razed by the sacriligious hand of an inhabitant; and the catacombs, containing the dust of many a celebrated member of the fraternity, torn up to furnish materials for fences, leaving us to guess at the situation they had occupied. The Rev. W. Ellis, then vicar, whose indignation at the circumstance was unbounded, wrote some Latin verses on the subject, expressive

of his sentiments; but they have been borne away by the stream of oblivion; and like the ashes of the hand that wrote them, they cannot be found.'

So the village lost part of its heritage. Rev Ellis did not live in Lastingham, being also vicar of Kirby Underbrow, and his hard-pressed curate, Jeremiah Carter, was too busy administering the parish and making ends meet to oppose the villagers.

The congregation continued to attend church and sing to the tune of at least one stringed instrument, namely a bass viol (which in 1795 is recorded as needing some new strings and a cover, costing ten shillings!)

In 1780 a trust was formed to administer Spaunton manor on behalf of Honoria Jenkins, who had inherited the house. One of the trustees was Henry Darley of Aldby Park, and thus began a family association with the manor which has continued until the present time.

Eight years after the formation of the trust, fields along Ings Lane were enclosed, and the village began to change, gradually growing to become as it is today.

Cockfighting and Witchcraft

Cockfighting was a common 18th century pursuit, and it has been suggested that fights were sometimes staged in the church crypt. Large scale formal events were certainly normal in York, as this advertisement from a 1791 York newspaper suggests:

York Cockings

The Long Main of Stags between H S Darley and John Wharton Esquires will be fought at the Cockpit without Bootham Bar in the York Spring Meeting 1791. To show 35 Stags on each side of the Main and 15 for the Bye Battles, for 10 gns. each Battle and 200 the main or odd battle. To weigh in on Saturday the 28th May and fight on Tuesday, Wednesday, Thursday and Friday following.

Feeders: Sunley for Mr Darley
Small for Mr Wharton

Belief in witches lasted well into the 18th century. Wise men and women supplied talismen to give protective charms for good purposes and spells for evil ones. Healing, apart from herbal medicines, was often faith healing, and the wise person combined a great knowledge of traditional skills and an innate gift for psychology with a long folk-memory dating back into pre-christian primitive times.

The Lastingham area had its fair share of witches. Some, like Bessy Ellis of Cropton and Mother Migg of Lastingham were good, others like Nan Skaife of Pickering were bad and greatly feared. The borderline between good and evil was always a very fine line, and the good were often blamed for being evil, serving as scapegoats for the community. (The last witch was burned in the nineteenth century). Some witches brewed and took hallucinatory drugs, which gave them the feeling of flying.

There are various signs and symbols which were commonly used by people in these times. A witch stone (sometimes called a Hag Stone) was a stone or pebble with a hole made by natural weathering. It hung by the door, window or chimney.

Crossed twigs of rowan over the barn door, or a twig carried in the pocket, was meant to ward off evil spirits. An old shoe put between the floorboards brought good luck when re-building or major renovations were undertaken. One was found in 1955 at the house now known as St Cedd's in High Street.

The bones of a favourite horse or cow were often buried near the house wall for good luck. One was found at Bridge Cottage, Front Street during repairs in 1972. Witch posts or witch stones were pots or stones placed near the hearth to prevent evil entering the room.

Often a 'bottery' (elderberry) bush was planted near the door to ward off evil spirits.

There were also charms, which in local dialect were called *"sigills"* (from the Latin *sigillae* - little grotesque figures of people and animals which were sold on December 20th, the feast of Sigillaria, the last day of the Roman Saturnalia. The feast was a cross between a fair and a carnival - 'the day of universal frolic and licence, the maddest, merriest day of the year').

CHAPTER FOUR

Some Lastingham Characters

Mother Migg of Lastingham

Mother Migg lived in Lastingham between around 1700 and 1750 - a local 'wise-woman', someone mid-way between a herbalist and a witch. Although there were apothecaries and surgeons about, modern medicine was in its infancy and people, especially in the country, would consult a wise woman (or man) when household remedies failed. She might well have made use of the natural mineral springs such as chalybeate on the moors, whose water contains carbonate of iron and is reputed to have tonic properties. The nearest is beyond the flatstones near Fairy Call Bridge on the way to Hutton, known as Loskey Spa.

Mother Migg had a good reputation and passed on her knowledge to future people of her kind. She got her name when, to quote the 19th century historian George Calvert, *'a demon threw her into 'a great slap o' mig'. For a great while after 'she stank prodigious so that none could with comfort draw nigh her'.*

Lastingham also had 'Cross Hob', (the only one known) an elf-like creature responsible for all kinds of mischief. Perhaps he is still here!

Henry Foster

Wesley's methodism began as a revival of personal religion with the aim of *'spreading scriptural holiness over the land.'* There was no departure by Wesley from the established church - it was the zeal with which the doctrines were taught, and the profession of godliness rather than the enjoyment of its power, that distinguished this new movement.

Methodism took root in the fertile ground of remote country areas, as did the Society of Friends, but links with the established church were maintained and many families belonged both to the established church and one of the other groups. There was a lot of Quaker activity in Lastingham - in 1743 there were twelve Quaker families in the parish, and meetings were held in their private houses, as well as in the licensed meeting house at Hutton-le-Hole.

John Wesley came several times to Yorkshire, including visits to York and to Scarborough, and people travelled many miles to his meetings and to hear him preach. There were other travelling preachers who succeeded in reaching remote districts both here and abroad. One such, Henry Foster, is buried in Lastingham churchyard, with the following epitaph:

NEAR THIS PLACE ARE DEPOSITED THE REMAINS OF HENRY FOSTER
WHO BY A SOLEMN COVENANT DEDICATION
OF HIMSELF TO GOD
MANIFESTED THAT HE WAS AN HEIR OF LIFE.
HE TRAVELLED AS A PREACHER IN THE CONNECTION
OF THE REV. JOHN WESLEY FOR 6 YEARS
IN THE TWO KINGDOMS OF ENGLAND AND IRELAND AFTER WHICH
HE RETURNED TO THIS VILLAGE
WORN OUT IN HIS MASTER'S SERVICE
WHERE HE RESIGNED HIS SOUL TO GOD
IN THE FULL TRIUMPH OF FAITH
ON THE TWELFTH DAY OF APRIL MDCCLXXXVII
IN THE FORTY THIRD YEAR OF HIS AGE

PSALM CXII v.6   DANIEL XII v.3   PSALM CXVI v.15

Jeremiah Carter

Jeremiah Carter was certainly curate at Lastingham from 1739 to 1764, possibly for longer. The vicar at the time was the Rev Luke Smelt who, though often absent, held the living for 62 years. He paid his curate £25 a year.

Carter wrote a letter replying to one from the Archdeacon questioning Carter's rather unusual methods of conducting his ministry:

It reads:

'I have a wife and thirteen children, and a stipend of £20 per annum, increased only by a few trifling surplice fees. I will not impose upon your understanding by attempting to advance any argument to show the impossibility of us all being supported from my church preferment. But I am fortunate enough to live in a neighbourhood where there are many rivulets which abound with fish, and being particularly partial to angling I am frequently so successful as to catch more than my family can consume while good, of which I make presents to the neighbouring gentry, all of whom are so generously grateful as to requite me with something else of seldom less value than two or threefold.

This is not all. My wife keeps a public house, and as my parish is so wide that some of my parishioners have to come from 10 to 15 miles to church, you will readily allow that some refreshment before they return must occasionally be necessary, and when can they have it more properly than when their journey is half performed?

Now sir, from your general knowledge of the world, I make

no doubt but you are well assured that the most general topics of conversation at public houses are politics and religion, with which ninety-nine out of one hundred of those who participate in the general clamour are totally unacquainted; and that perpetually ringing in the ears of a pastor who has the welfare and happiness of his flock at heart must be no small mortification.

To divert their attention from these foibles over their cups I take down my violin and play them a few tunes, which gives me an opportunity of seeing that they get no more liquor than is necessary for refreshment; and if the young people propose a dance, I seldom answer in the negative; nevertheless, when I announce time for return, they are ever ready to obey my commands, and generally with the donation of a sixpence they shake hands with my children, and bid God bless them. Thus my parishioners enjoy a triple advantage, being instructed, fed and amused at the same time. Moreover, this method of spending their Sunday is so congenial with their inclinations, that they are imperceptibly led along the paths of piety and morality, whereas, in all probability, the most exalted discourses, followed with no variety but heavenly contemplations, would pass like the sounds of harmony over an ear incapable of discerning the distinction of sounds.'

This reply was apparently considered quite satisfactory!

John Jackson RA

John Jackson was born in Lastingham in 1778, the son of the village tailor. Apprenticed to his father, Jackson spent an increasing amount of time drawing portraits and miniatures of the customers he visited on his father's business, and so came to the notice of the Marquis of Normanby at Mulgrave Castle, near Whitby. His Lordship was a patron of the arts, and arranged for Jackson to be provided with an allowance to study at the Royal Academy.

Living in London, Jackson justified his patrons' support, becoming a Royal Academician in 1817. Visiting Lastingham (which he would often reach by sea via Whitby) every year after the Summer Exhibition, he used his musical talents in arranging hymns for the methodist chapel, of which he had been a trustee since 1804.

In 1824 Jackson designed and began a series of repairs and improvements to Lastingham's dilapidated church. The only surviving evidence of this work is his copy of Correggio's *Christ in the Garden*, painted as an altar piece, now hanging in the tower.

John Jackson in his church

A well-liked and respected member of the Academy, Jackson had been due to be elected President, when he died of tuberculosis in 1831. There is an inscribed stone in memory of him on the downstream side of Jackson Bridge in Low Street.

Jackson Bridge

CHAPTER FIVE

19th Century

In 1824 there was a population of 225 in Lastingham, which by 1872 had only increased by 5. It is known that the population of the area increased considerably in 1856 with the opening of the iron workings at Rosedale, and that some of the miners lived in Lastingham. Most of them however congregated in Rosedale itself; some were Irish, others Scottish.

Joseph Farington was a diarist and traveller, and in order to get the feel of rural life in the nineteenth century it is interesting to read an entry in his diary, written en route from London to Scotland on 7 September 1801:

> 'At Kirkbymoorside we found a most clean and comfortable inn where we had an excellent breakfast - here I met with a very intelligent farmer who gave me much information.
>
> He spoke as others have done of the harvest being abundant and excellent, and said the markets had been lowered in the proportion of from 16 to 18 shillings and even a guinea - to which high prices they have been advanced - to ten shillings, but he added that he did not believe they would be permanent. He said it was at present owing to the little farmers being obliged, in order to answer demands upon them, to bring their corn to market, but when their sale is over the strong farmers as he called them, those who hold £800 or £1,000 a year in their hands, will keep back their stock and only deal it out at prices agreed among themselves.

He said farmers of this description do now even purchase from the little farmers at the reduced prices with the above view. The country banks he said will be the ruin of the country, for by their assistance the farmers can carry into execution these speculations.

It is a great evil, he observed, that any farmer of so large an amount as £800 should be allowed by the landlords. Were they limited to £150 or £200 a year the public would soon feel a sensible difference in many essential respects.

The price of day labour at Kirkbymoorside is one shilling a day and find victuals, or two shillings without victuals. Some work for 18 pence. In harvest time the labourers avail themselves of the necessity of the farmers, and have from 30 pence to five shillings a day'.

In 1840 St Cedd's well, in the main street of Lastingham, was given a canopy made with stone from Rosedale Abbey. (As we have seen, the stones from Lastingham monastery had already been used up in building new farms and restoring houses, much to the disgust of Ellis, the vicar of the time).

Local travel was becoming easier. The present Wellington Bridge, on the way to Askew, replaced the ford over Lastingham Beck and was named to commemorate the death of the Duke of Wellington in 1852.

Wellington Bridge

On the Hutton road, Fairy Call Bridge over Loskey Beck was completed in 1890, and got its name because the fairies were said to blow out the carriage lamps as you passed by, the wind being channelled between the high banks to the east of the bridge.

In 1887 a new road was laid leading up Lidsty Hill, and a cross was erected to commemorate Queen Victoria's Jubilee. Until the 1980s, the manor forester would, at the request of the Court Leet, cut a swathe in the saplings near the cross so that it could see and be seen by the village - a small refinement of village life that has now been abandoned.

Before the new road, the route south out of the village had previously consisted of a narrow track (still in existence) towards Spaunton, and coffins had to be brought down the track on wooden sleds such as were used for carting peat. This was the most direct route from Spaunton to the churchyard. The only road from Lastingham to Appleton had previously been via Askew and Hamley Lane - a long way round.

In 1892 it was decided to supply the village with piped spring water, and a system of collection and storage tanks was installed. There was however no sewage system, and waste was either burnt, buried or tipped into the beck just as it always had been. Each cottage valued its access to the beck, with its trout which were then bigger than they are now. The vicar was able to turn his tap on for the first time in 1903.

A Wake or Spring Fair continued to be held during the century. The historian Weston, writing in 1914, refers to it as having been 'held annually within living memory'.

Three severe winters were recorded in the Lastingham area during the 19th century. These were in 1878-9, 1882-3 and 1894-5, the last being the worst when 'snow of great volume swept across the moors.'

Jack Todd

'Jackie' lived at Bainwood on the way to Hutton, and for many years looked after a pack of 15 or 20 couples of harriers for "Squire" Shepherd of Douthwaite Dale between Hutton and Kirkbymoorside. The hounds were well regarded in hunting circles.

After "Squire" Shepherd died in poor circumstances, Bridge Cottage was sold together with land and other properties to defray his funeral expenses and pay his debts. Jackie Todd kept the pack going, helped by Jack Parker from Sinnington. Todd was riding to hounds on a donkey at the age of 87, and died 'at an advanced age' in 1903,

One of Jack's sons, Jim Todd, was a carrier taking things to and from Kirkbymoorside by horse and cart. He would come to the

Square at the junction of High Street, Low Street and Front Street, and blow his hunting horn in order to attract custom.

Henry Todd, another son or grandson of Jackie, lived in Lastingham at a later date. He was a catcher of rabbits, rats and other pests. One of the 1940 evacuees remembers being frightened by the day's catch, which *'lay at the bottom of the stairs, and all those little eyes seemed to be watching you'*.

The Rev Robert Harrison

From 1828 until he died in 1850 the Rev Harrison was the Vicar of Lastingham. He was much respected and built a new school in the village, while also enlarging the vicarage where his initials are carved on the lintel of the front door. He died aged 78, and is buried in the churchyard.

His curate, the Rev Montagu, described him as:

> *'a man beyond the average; an excellent agriculturalist and judge of stock. Frequently consulted by Lord Feversham (of Helmsley) - a noted short-horn breeder - in selection and breeding... My dear old vicar, Harrison, with his long hoe and staff, and a black-cock feather in his hat'*.

Montagu was curate for two and a half years between 1841 and 1844. He lived in the cottage (now Ivy Cottage in High Street) built by Harrison especially for him, and wrote of it:

> *'It was all on the ground floor, and situated on the west side of the road leading northward onto the moor; and had facing it a*

delightful spring of pure water. I rented some meadows between my
house and the beck for my horse'.

Montagu also mentions *'the tiny trout'* he caught in the *'sweet
little beck'.* He subsequently became Rector at Hawkwell, retired
aged over 81 and died at Rochford aged 96.

Church Renovations

In 1817 the vicarage at Lastingham had been enlarged and
roofed with tiles. St Mary Church had not seen any major
restoration since the 16th century and was in a poor state.

In 1828 the artist John Jackson initiated a programme of
church renovation. This included the paving of the floor, re-
roofing, and the installation of boxed pews and an altar piece, all
in the latest Georgian fashion. Unfortunately the renovations
were not carried out quite to the artist's specifications, and
within fifty years the roof was leaking again.

The Jackson family were converts to Methodism, and John
Jackson senior gave the village land for the building of a
methodist chapel in Low Street, now closed. He was a precentor
and circuit steward.

Anne Darley, who was the daughter of the lord of the manor,
had married the London physician Dr Sydney Ringer. They
bought a farm near Lastingham church and converted it into a
holiday home (the house now known as St Mary's). At a
birthday party for their seven year old daughter Annie, the child
choked to death on a cherry stone, and the tragedy prompted
the Ringers to embark on a major new restoration of the church.
This was begun in 1879, during which the building was re-

floored and re-roofed, and new windows were installed, mostly as memorials to Annie.

The architect for the Ringer restoration was J L Pearson, who designed Christ Church at the nearby village of Appleton, and also Truro Cathedral. It is to him that we owe the beauty of the present interior of Lastingham's church. The cost to Dr Ringer was about £4,000, towards which the Ecclesiastical Commissioners contributed £500.

In the church there is a piece of sculpture known as the 'Baroque Calvary' which was originally on board the Spanish ship *Salvadore del Mundo*, which surrendered to the *Victory* off Cape St Vincent, Portugal, in 1797. Admiral Rodney's secretary, a Devon man, left it to a Lastingham family, and Sir Cyril Fuller later gave it to the church.

Before 1859 church music was provided by a variety of instruments, but in 1857 an appeal was launched in Lastingham for £105 to buy a small organ. This was installed in the church two years later.

There is a window in the north aisle of Lastingham church commemorating the death in Bangalore, at the age of 21, of 2nd Lieut Ralph James Ross serving with the 4th Madras Pioneers at the time of the Indian Mutiny.

In 1871 the church tithes were changed to money instead of produce and in 1897 Mrs Fox and the Flintoft family together bought an extension to the churchyard at one shilling (5p) a yard. The Archbishop of York came to consecrate the ground.

School Building

In 1836 a village school was built in Low Street by the Rev Robert Harrison, with the vicar as sole trustee. It came to be classed as a National School under the 1870 Education Act which for the first time provided that there was to be compulsory education for all children over the age of five. (Schools set up by non-conformists were not classed as National Schools, and were generally owned by the British and Foreign Schools Society).

In 1884 the teachers in Lastingham village school were Mr & Mrs Hutchcroft, who were well liked, and who were Methodists. By then the Reverend Easterby was vicar and sole trustee, and the school log book shows that all was not well:

> 'Schoolwork resumed this morning in another bulding. Owing to a dispute between the Vicar and the Managers, the Vicar refuses to deliver up the keys of the Schoolroom to the Managers and prohibits the schoolmaster from entering the school premises'.

The vicar then appointed his own teacher, whereupon the Hutchcrofts took the children down the road to the chapel and continued to teach them there, and the vicar's school was closed. Arthur Hutchcroft, however, continued to take the Sunday School and remained the church organist. Sixteen years later, in April 1900, the Hutchcrofts left the village to go to Sinnington school.

In 1885 a new school was built at the bottom of Lidsty Hill in memory of Harriet Louisa Darley, to cater for 80 children, but the average roll was about 40.

Eventually the old schoolroom in Low Street became the village Reading Room containing 600 volumes when it opened in 1890, of which only 120 were still there by 1905. The property is now a holiday cottage. The new school closed before the Second World War but was reopened for evacuees, finally closing in 1943 when the building was let to the village at a peppercorn rent for use as a village hall.

Violent Deaths

In 1882 a man called Robert Charter, who worked for a family called Wood at Cropton, was living in Lastingham in a house on the site now occupied partly by Quern Cottage and partly by the Old School House next to the village hall (which at that time was still the school).

Charter spread a story that Joseph Wood and his nine-year-old grandson were emigrating to Canada, and then forged a letter purporting to be from Wood to his family at Cropton, post-marked Liverpool from where it had been posted by a relative of Charter's who was in fact emigrating. No-one therefore worried unduly when Wood and his grandson disappeared, but eventually suspicions were aroused. Wood's body was found buried in a field along Ings Lame (now the sewage works). The body of the grandchild was never found, but was rumoured to have been chopped up and fed to the pigs.

Charter was charged with murder and brought before the Pickering magistrates in December, with his son-in-law William Hardwick who was charged with harbouring a murderer.

At the ensuing trial at York Assizes in March 1873 Hardwick

was acquitted, but, although there was not enough evidence to convict him of murder, Charter was imprisoned for twenty years. As a result the villagers gathered together to pull down his house, so clearing the site for the buildings now standing on it. After his release Charter became a preacher, and later died a pauper in a 'poor house'.

One anonymous rhyme about Charter reads:

'No one pities old Bob Charter
For that deed that he has done,
For he killed the poor old farmer
And his helpless little son'.

Two suicides are also recorded during the century - one man hanged himself at Brook Farm in Low Street, and another shot himself in the barn on Cropton Lane.

Charter's house being pulled down

CHAPTER SIX

Parish Government

Local government has existed for centuries, and whilst changes have occurred from time to time, the general pattern of the present system was firmly established just one hundred years ago, although some of its general features are quite ancient.

In the Middle Ages, England consisted of a number of counties, each of which was divided into several hundreds, and these, in their turn, contained a number of manors. The rural parish of the present day is in many cases identical with the ancient manor.

Edward III appointed Commissioners of the Peace in each county, who soon became known as Justices of the Peace. Their duties were quite embracing, and increased as time went on. They held courts for the trial of minor offences, and in this capacity the Justices were magistrates. They met four times a year in Quarter Session, and at these meetings they transacted the business of the county area and directed its affairs. Practically every landowner was a Justice of the Peace, so that the government of the counties was entirely in the hands of the landed gentry. This system of county government lasted until 1888, although many ancient towns had charters and were self-governing.

For many purposes, however, the parish was the unit of local government. By the Poor Law of 1601, each parish was made responsible for the maintenance of its own poor.

In 1834, the Poor Law was amended, and the parishes were

grouped into unions. An entirely new grouping, having no relationship to the hundreds, was adopted, and Lastingham was included in the Pickering union. In 1848 a central Board of Health was established, with power to divide counties into sanitary districts, urban and rural, and again the power was exercised with a total disregard of the existing areas.

Until 1894, there were no civil parishes and parish government was through the church Vestry - not always democratically elected - and there is a long history dating back to Elizabethan times and before, when each parish had its own officers such as the Constable, the Surveyor of Highways and the Overseers of the Poor. The County Councils (in Yorkshire, the three Ridings) and county boroughs were created by the Local Government Act, 1888 and the completion of the pattern was the creation of urban and rural districts (which had previously existed as Sanitary Districts under the Public Health Acts) and the parishes. The civil parish was an identifiable area serving people within a community small enough for local people to be able to control and to understand its workings. Thus Lastingham, Spaunton, Appleton-le-Moors, Hutton-le-Hole, Rosedale and others all became civil parishes over one hundred years ago.

Larger parishes have to have an elected parish council, but smaller parishes such as Lastingham need only have parish meetings. The Parish Meeting is the most democratic form of local government in the whole country. The parish is, therefore, accorded a unique place in local government, albeit with limited powers and despite several local government reorganisations. Since 1894, when the Gladstone government passed the British

Councils Act, parishes have survived in more or less their present form.

The parish with its relatively small area, is the most tried and tested of all local government administrative units. Since Elizabethan times, the parish has been the basic administrative area for the Poor Law and this continued until 1834 when Boards of Guardians were formed. The parish was also used by both church and state as an area for tax collection.

Nowadays the parish has a number of minor powers and duties. The powers, often subject to agreement by landowners, other bodies, agencies and the District or County Councils, include provision of car and cycle parks, public toilets, street lighting (at extra local cost), open spaces including village greens, planting of roadside verges, new and existing rights of way, seats and shelters, litter bins, allotments, sports and recreational facilities, village halls, entertainments, arts and tourism, flagpoles, public clocks, burial grounds, war memorials, non-ecclesiastical charities, village ponds and the opportunity of commenting on planning applications.

The Manor of Spaunton

Spaunton and Lastingham were both part of the manor and, though different, are often grouped together - two small villages, one on top of the hill with its manor house and the other in the valley with its ancient church. Today Spaunton is the smaller of the two but in the past it was a much larger settlement.

Flint implements from the Stone and Bronze Ages have been found and there is an interesting causeway linking two parts of the pathway between Spaunton and Lastingham. The life of Spaunton seems to have centred round the peaceful pursuit of farming.

We have the first detailed account of a manor in the Domesday survey of 1086 when the first lord, Gamel, was in possession of lands in Yorkshire, Derbyshire, Lincolnshire and Cheshire. Gamel appears to have been deposed in favour of Berenger de Todeni, who gave land at Lastingham to Stephen, who was also given land and the lordship of the manor by the king. After moving to York, Abbot Stephen kept control of the manor lands, which were gradually extended by gifts to the church.

The manor included the Forest of Spaunton, described in 1328 as *'between the rivers Dove and Seven, and between the boundary of Cleveland in the north and the road leading through Catthwait from Pickering to Helmsley'*. The game in the forest, however, belonged to the king until 1335, when the king agreed to transfer the gaming rights to the abbot (in exchange for other interests), but only after ascertaining that the game was not very plentiful!

At the time of the suppression of the monasteries, the church remained with St Mary's in York, while the manor was acquired by Lord Grey de Wilton.

De Wilton only kept the manor six years before selling to the Bonvell family, from whom it passed through the generations until a trust was formed in 1770, one of whose members was Henry Darley of Aldby Park. The manor then passed down through the family to the present George Winn-Darley.

Large areas of open space within the parish of Lastingham and Spaunton are therefore under the ownership of the manor.

Forestry, fishing, shooting, quarrying and farming all contribute to the maintenance of the land. The manor boundary is marked by fifteen boundary stones, and each new lord of the manor walks round the boundary carrying the manor banner, accompanied by such officials as the forester and pinder, and the holders of common rights. This was done three times during the 20th century, in 1910, 1956 and 1987.

Although most of the houses one can now see are 18th century or later, Woodman's Cottage has a stone dated 1695 and is an excellent example of a 'long house'. It was thatched until about 1915 and was a 13th/14th century dwelling house. Old photographs show a pond opposite the Manor Cottages and the New Inn was licensed until 1969. Though the village has no chapel, services were at one time held at Hill Top Farm.

Spaunton's pinfold is still in place, and a pinder is still in fact appointed by the Court Leet.

The Darley Arabian

Although in the early eighteenth century horse racing had not yet reached the height of its popularity, it was a sport favoured by many from royalty to the less well-off. British bloodstock has long been admired by those interested in fine horses, and in 1940 7,000 brood mares could trace their ancestry back to the three founding stallions: The Bayerley Turk, The Godolphin Arabian, and The Darley Arabian,

Thomas Darley of Aldby Park had a position as a consular official in Aleppo (in Syria, then part of the Ottoman Empire), and offered to buy the handsome arab stallion he admired, but he was refused. With the aid of friends, he therefore kidnapped the horse and smuggled it out of the country and back to England in 1704.

There was no official outcry, but shortly afterwards Thomas Darley's body, with those of his companions, was found in a dark alley in Aleppo. Some sources say he had been poisoned, others that he had been stabbed to death. Either way, it was murder, and the culprits were never found.

Common Rights

Common rights originated in pre-mediaeval times, and the purpose for which they were given differed in the manor of Spaunton from that in many other parts of the country.

Here the rights were given to those with no land of their own, to enable them to have a basic means of feeding themselves and their families. Rights were 'sheep gaits', but they could be used for other animals. For example, one sheep gait was equal to one breeding ewe with followers or 3 geese or 3 ducks; 8 sheep gaits equalled 1 head of cattle, 1 donkey or 1 horse with a follower of up to 1 year old.

The situation was changed in 1979 after a public enquiry when, in spite of a large volume of written evidence and many objections, several householders were deprived of their inherited rights by the Commons Commission.

peat gathering

Apart from grazing rights the common-right holder could also cut peat for his own fire, cut and take away bracken for his own use, or take top stones for repairing his own buildings. There were also 'garths' where potatoes could be grown (there are some still on the moor now, used either as field, or - along the road to Bank Foot - for vegetables).

Local rights were controlled by the Court Leet consisting of a foreman and twelve jurymen who met once a year. Any encroachment on common land without the consent of the Court would lead to fines. Should the fine be ignored the members of the Court would take direct action, for example by removing unauthorised fencing.

the Court Leet in action

Though times have changed, the manor still performs an important function in preseving the continued life of the moors and woodland and green grassy spaces within its boundaries.

CHAPTER SEVEN

Lastingham Mill and Joseph Foord

The road bridge in Lastingham's Front Street spans Ellers Beck, not to be confused with the more prestigious Eller Beck with its several waterfalls which runs north through Beck Hole and on into Eskdale. Ellers Beck descends into Lastingham first through three pastures, and then through the gardens at St. Mary's, and past the site of the old mill to reach the bridge, after which it becomes Ings Beck. Above the pastures where the moor begins, however, it is forded by the transverse footpath from Hartoft through to Hutton-le-Hole, and here, even on early maps, it appears as Hole Beck back to its source two miles to the north on Spaunton Moor.

The water reaching the road-bridge is supplemented by a small stream from the north-west, which runs through a tunnel under the garden of the Blacksmith's Arms, to emerge through a concealed exit not visible from the road, between Anserdale Lane and the garden boundary of The Mill House. There it joins Ellers Beck below the garden bridge and the arched flume from the original wheel-house, both waters mingling for the final eighty yards down to the road bridge.

At first sight it seems strange that neither Ellers Beck nor this concealed inflow ever played any part in working the great 14 foot water-wheel once driving the corn mill at Lastingham. The water rights for the beck were for a fulling mill, probably at Askew. ('Fulling' was the process of cleansing and thickening cloth by pressing it between rollers and cleaning it with soap or 'fuller's earth'). What then actually drove the Lastingham corn mill? The answer to this apparent mystery is probably connected with the work of the remarkable 18th century Yorkshireman, Joseph Foord.

Foord's speciality, regarded by some as near-genius, was to tap existing moorland watercourses, and by means of meticulously routed channels and aqueducts to furnish the higher moorland villages and pastures with a permanent water supply. He had noted that the high plateau of the North York Moors has an overall and steady tilt downwards from west to east. By acute self-taught surveying, he was able to pinpoint exactly where he could either divert or tap existing streams. As long as even a slight overall incline existed, his team would dig and cut in precisely observed cooperation with the land-fall, thus enabling a steady flow of water to be provided by gravity.

What may be Foord's most easterly watercourse was cut late in the 18th century, taking water from Loskey Beck on the west face of Spaunton Moor, north of Hutton-le-Hole. The beck was tapped at a point about a mile due north of Fairy Call Bridge on the Hutton-le-Hole to Lastingham road. Now no longer in use, but still discernible throughout its length, this water-course runs south-south-east past Bainwood Head Farm, skirting the southern edge of High Cross Plain and Camomile Farm, to reach Lastingham some two miles from its source. If not Foord's own handwork, this Lastingham watercourse suggests someone closely connected with or influenced by him.

It was created solely to operate the water-wheel of the new stone-built mill at the end of the 18th century.

The Mill-Race

From its source down to and past Bainwood Head Farm, and under the main road beyond, the watercourse is all a man-made channel or 'drain', and one of exceptional length. On the south of the road, it runs due east to the foot of Spaunton Bank, and over the years has furrowed its own small stream-bed which probably needed little further manual improvement until it reached Lastingham. On maps dated as early as 1890 it appears as a small beck in its own right, remaining unnamed on one edition, but dubbed simply 'mill-race' on another. For its last half-mile to Lastingham, it is slightly augmented by several rivulets draining the moor and pastures north of the road.

Just to the east of Holywell House there is tucked under the roadside bank of the mill-race, and so concealed from passers-by, one of the least known of the wells of Lastingham, Mary Magdalene's Well. This seems to fill its modest basin of clear spring water from the hills above. Certainly it lies to the south of the mill race but its source is unknown.

On the edge of Lastingham village, below Camomile Farm, the mill-race used to fill a small reservoir pool built to sustain the mill in times of scant supply. The pool was drained in 1900 after two local children, Ernest Parker and his sister Annie Elizabeth, were found drowned in its six feet of water, and the mill was ultimately closed down.

Below the site of the pool, what is left of the old mill-race continues past the gates of St. Mary's on the left, then drops to run beside the road and into the tunnel under the beer-garden at the Blacksmith's Arms, emerging to join Ellers Beck above the road bridge.

The mill was driven by water diverted along a gulley cut through what is now the garden of St. Mary's, to a small elongated mill-pond and thence, controlled by a penstock, to plunge down to work the wheel of the mill, thereafter emerging through the arched flume, still intact to this day, to join Ellers Beck in the garden of The Mill House.

Though not required for the mill after its closure, the flow was harnessed for a while after World War 1 to work a small dynamo providing a limited electricity supply to the Mill House and its various out-buildings. One of the out-buildings, now the house on the green, was the mill's wagon shed and store.

The metal machinery was removed from the mill to help with the war effort in 1939-45.

the Mill House

CHAPTER EIGHT

The Twentieth Century

The century opened for Lastingham with the installation of a clock in the church tower in 1901. The clock was officially started by a Mrs Pulleyne who was a member of a York family that had village connections at this time. Whether the lady climbed up the vertical ladder in the tower to perform the task is not known. Much later in the 1980s the mechanism was connected to the electricity supply by an anonymous donor in order to avoid such a climb. However, twice a year the climb has still to be performed today in order to adjust the clock to and from British summer time.

In 1902 for the coronation of Edward VII the village planted a pink chestnut tree at the west end of the churchyard. Telephone lines were installed in 1903.

Houses in Lastingham were in the past more numerous but smaller than at present. The last thatched dwelling - an old long house on the site of the present Ovins Well House - was demolished some time during the early part of the 20th century, and other old decaying cottages have been rejuvenated over the years and given a new life.

A plan for a Lastingham and Rosedale Light Railway linked to the North-Eastern's Pickering-Helmsley-Gilling line had been rejected in 1897 because of lack of public need, and further proposals were made in the early 1900s when it was pointed out that the area was rich in ironstone, flagstone, freestone, shale and china clay, 'all of which could be exploited with the benefit of railway access.' Nearly half the land for the railway was offered to the company set up to build it, but after initial work had begun and the first sod ceremonially cut with a silver spade, the necessary finance did not materialise and the plans were dropped just before the start of the Great War. According to local folk-lore, the silver spade had disappeared without trace.

There are two memorials in Lastingham to those who served in the 1914-18 war. One is in the form of a stone plaque on the east boundary of the churchyard, commemorating those men from Lastingham and Spaunton who served in the war - among whom one of the Flintoft brothers had been decorated with the *Croix de Guerre*. The other memorial is a cross made of lealholm stone, the design having been taken from stone fragments in the church crypt. This is in the churchyard on the right of the main entrance path. It is here that the poppy wreath is laid on November 11th each year.

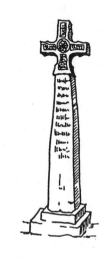

There is no memorial to the 1939-45 war; the men in the village were either too old, too young or in reserved occupations at the time. Lastingham was not affected by enemy action during the 1939-45 war but Spaunton was. The remnants of entrench-ments can still be seen on the moor as the area was a training ground for troops. Since the war, several sweeps have been carried out to remove war-time debris, and a few small fragments can sometimes still be seen.

In 1987, after heavy rain, a hand grenade was discovered wedged in the bank of Ellers Beck, in the corner between the bridge and the wall of Bridge Cottage. Identified as a First World War grenade, it was exploded on the moor. It had been stored and brought out again for training purposes during the Second World War, and left unnoticed on the moor until the rains washed it down.

Another grenade had been found some years earlier by a boy, who kept it in his toy box and used it as a football, until one day he threw it and blew a hole in the Reading Room wall. Luckily no one was hurt.

The blacksmith's shop in Spaunton was demolished by a bomb jettisoned from an aircraft during the war and one person died. Tom Strickland's uncle was preparing to open the door of his house nearby when the blast blew in the door and killed him.

Two aircraft collided over the village of Appleton le Moors. One aircraft dived into a clay pit with such force that the machine was left there and the pit filled in. Also imprinted in the clay was the shape of a man with an arm and leg missing. A few weeks later someone found a human thumb while cleaning a blocked gutter.

A number of evacuees (originally 39) came to Lastingham during the Second World War, and the recently closed school was re-opened for them. Some returned home when it was thought there was no immediate danger of invasion, some stayed on after the war, and some still re-visit the village - all speak well of the happy times they had during those troubled years.

Before the First World War the Pulleyn family gave parties at

Christmas for the children. They employed local help when they were holidaying in Lastingham during the summer and one of these 'maids' related this story when she returned to Lastingham as an elderly lady some years ago. In Queen Victoria's Jubilee year the Pulleyns and all their staff went to London for the event and the young local girl was put in the care of the cook who, fond of her gin, placed the girl on one of the public stands and went off to have a drink. But the girl saw very little of the procession, as a man in a big black 'stove-pipe hat' came to sit near her and she was terrified because she thought he was Jack the Ripper!

At this time there were two half holidays from school in the spring, one to pick snowdrops and one to pick primroses at the Vicarage, followed by tea and buns in each case. Gypsies came to Farndale for the daffodils, and after picking and bunching them, brought them to the villages to sell. There was also a Sunday school outing.

In the spring a stallion belonging to a farmer called Sonley would be groomed and decked out with ribbons and bells. It would be taken to Kirkbymoorside on market days and walked round the villages, and bookings would be taken from anyone who had a mare to foal. Everyone turned out to see the horse 'because it was a handsome sight'.

In 1930 (until 1966) Stan Crosby owned the Blacksmith's Arms. He sometimes played his fiddle for the customers, and his wife served delicious teas with ham and eggs to week-end tourists who walked or cycled to the village - there were fewer cars about in those days.

Before the Second World War, there was a forge near the

Blacksmiths Arms, with a small wooden hut at one end for the postman. He brought letters by bicycle from Kirkbymoorside, delivered them, repaired to his little hut to eat his sandwiches, emptied the letter-box and returned to Kirkbymoorside with the outgoing mail.

the Blacksmith's Arms

A Mr Sheldon ran a youth hostel for a short time at St Cedds at the bottom of High Street and a previous resident, Mr Bygate held musical evenings in the drawing room. Sweets were sold from the window of the house on the green.

Until very recently, nettle beer was made in the spring from the young nettle tops 'to clear out the system after the winter'. Gale beer (made from bog-myrtle) was used as a refreshing drink later in the year.

Seeds of root crops were sown when the moon was waning, and the seeds of leafy vegetables when the moon was waxing. This was an old Eastern tradition brought to Europe at the time of the Moorish invasions, or some say the crusades.

Doorsteps were not scrubbed until the Easter spring cleaning - if they were cleaned before 'they only got mucky again'.

In 1936 the centenary of the opening of the first school was celebrated by a party in the grounds. The old reading room was converted into a house in 1970, but the Womens Institute rescued the clock and installed it in the wall of the village hall near the entrance.

Severe winters occurred from time to time. The whole country was affected in 1939-40 when Lastingham was cut off for two months. Horse drawn ploughs could not cope with the volume of snow. When the butcher's van managed to get as far as the top of Lidsty Hill, the butcher was able to get out and put his cap on the top of a telegraph pole protruding from the snow.

William Featherstone, who lived at Mount Pleasant (now Ovins Well House), supplied milk to the babies and young children, and water from his well (St Ovin's Well) in times of drought.

Scouts and guides regularly came for summer camps in the field at Bankfoot, and one year the scouts widened Tranmire Beck on the moor to create a swimming pool. Though still remembered as the scout pool, it has since been spoilt by winter flooding and destruction of the dam.

Water now comes to the village from East Ness and there is a small pumping station at the foot of Lidsty Hill. Before the arrival of mains drainage or piped water, one of the houses in High Street had a 'flush toilet' situated in a large cupboard near the front door. Ash was taken from the fire to another cupboard upstairs, which fell through a trap-door into the bowl in the cupboard below when the chain was pulled.

The Second World War was a turning point for the 20th century and village life changed. Electricity was installed in 1948 but mains drainage arrived only in 1969. During the digging of the drains, a passage was found leading from the Blacksmith's Arms to the beck, awakening folk-memories of the monks having an avenue of escape from the church in time of danger. Whether they did or not, the passage was in fact an old sewer!

A police house was built. The prospect of heavy traffic and itinerant labour in connection with the proposed reservoir in Farndale had made a police presence desirable, and the house was retained until after the plans for the reservoir (first mooted in the 1930s) were abandoned in 1971. The house (Willow Garth, on Ings Lane) is now privately owned.

A number of events were organised in 1963-4 to provide a new organ for the church, and the Lastingham Exhibition in 1963 is still remembered. Volunteers had to sleep in the village hall overnight as a security precaution to protect items which people had loaned for the display.

The winter of 1978-79 was a severe one but the village was only cut off for two days over the weekend. In 1986 flash floods affected a considerable area between Kirkbymoorside and Lastingham, and Ellers Beck overflowed to flood the road near the green. Some houses in the village were damaged, large trees up-rooted, and a great deal of debris washed down from the high ground.

Royal events such as coronations were marked in the usual way - holidays from school and the presentation of mugs to children. The village also celebrated the Queen's jubilee in 1978. A pink-flowering hawthorn was planted on the green for the Jubilee.

In 1978 the 900th anniversary of the church that Stephen built was celebrated modestly with a musical recital and a flower festival, and an exhibition of village history in the village hall.

Another tree was planted in 1990 in Low Street to commemorate the 75th anniversary of the founding of the Womens' Institute movement. A local group of the W.I. was formed in 1946, but after a lively half century disbanded at the end of 1999 because of falling numbers.

In 1989 a number of buildings and other structures were registered as listed buildings, and so are likely to be preserved in their present state.

In the same year the village shop, which had moved round the corner from Lastingham Lodge into Low Street, closed with the post office it contained. A small community post office operated from the Blacksmiths Arms until 1999, and otherwise the village continued to be well served with travelling amenities.

the village shop

70

The laundry, newspapers, milk, fish and meat still come in this year 2000, as do the mobile library and the school bus; but the grocer retired three or four years ago and the garage and petrol pump have long been gone. The Blacksmiths Arms survives them!

In 1990 most of the lead was stolen from the roof of the church and had to be replaced. A successful appeal was launched for further funds for the maintenance of and improvements to the church and crypt, and for the renewal of churchyard lighting.

The village hall continues to be used for village events, meetings, concerts, art exhibitions and the like, and residents meet in the hall on a regular basis for morning coffee and village chat.

Since the formation of the National Park and the designation of the village as within a Conservation Area, many more visitors come to see the church and the village. Lastingham has largely become a holiday and retirement retreat, though it still benefits from the existence of two working farms, and there are a number of people living in the village who are in full or part time employment in the area or further afield.

The end of the century and of the millennium was celebrated with an informal midnight service in the crypt and a modest party in the village hall, with plenty of fireworks in evidence throughout the evening. By way of lasting memorials, Mary Magdalene Well was given a low stone arch incorporating the existing stone inscription, and an inscribed millennium stone was  erected on the edge of the moor at the top of High Street. A short dedication service was held around the millennium stone on New Year's Day, followed by a walk over the moor which ended with a convivial lunch in the village hall, as a fitting start to the new century.

Lastingham Village